TOM - THE CAT

TOM - THE CAT

The Life and Work of Tom Cat in Sonnets

ELIZABETH REINACH

Library of Congress Control Number:		2019908819
ISBN:	Hardcover	978-1-9845-9053-4
	Softcover	978-1-9845-9051-0
	eBook	978-1-9845-9052-7

Print information available on the last page.

Rev. date: 07/01/2019

To order additional copies of this book, contact:
Xlibris
800-056-3182
www.Xlibrispublishing.co.uk
Orders@Xlibrispublishing.co.uk
796442

CONTENTS

DRAMATIS PERSONAE

Animals

Tom—large male tabby cat
Candice—female pedigree cat
Neighbour's cat—female cat
Scott—dog next door
Morgan—an elderly female cat
Ten Bible Beasts

Narrator—manager and financial consultant who has many friends and contacts

In narrator's household

Narrator's wife—fifty years old
Maid—works for narrator's wife
Tom

To the memory of Koshka, who lives forever in my mind

ACKNOWLEDGEMENTS

Aberdeen Writers' Circle and Lemon Tree Writers' Group
for all their help and encouragement at meetings

Keith Murry for inspiring and criticising the project work

The Tom the Cat sonnets are modelled on Shakespeare's sonnets, although the content is very different.

The first line of each sonnet is the first line of a Shakespeare sonnet.

TYRANT CHILD

Thou art as tyranneous, so as thou art,
My tyrant came in a baby's rug.
A spirit from the Bard or from Plutarch,
The kit was given to me for my first hug.

We placed him in a basket, with a pillow,
Milk to drink, a blue shawl, and a bonnet.
He curled and made the pillow hollow,
My muse I watched, and I wrote a sonnet.

His each miaow became my call to class,
His tyranny became my sonnet's muse.
Called like a devotee to Roman Mass,
I write each day a sonnet as he mews.

Tom is the tyrant who compels my verse,
Great souls overhung his cradle at birth.

SUMMER BIRTH

Can I compare thee to a Summer's day?
Grass, sweet as fresh legumes, which tastes the best,
Soft blues, Summer banquets from sky and bay,
A ripening world, swelling to Autumn's harvest.

And you, Tom, wriggling through grass and fern,
On a criminal quest, your cloak of fur,
And your death's claws plying like the devil's churn,
How do you find a place in Summer's lure?

Tom is the killer of a sweet Summer's day,
And cannot be compared with hopeful green,
With barbs to murder Spring, he finds his way,
Destroying all new life, babes still to wean.

Yet Tom too was born in Summertime,
An infamous rogue, I made him mine.

BEDROOM TRYST

Weary with toil, I haste me to my bed,
Turn back the sheets and slide like setting sun,
Unwind my coil, stretch out each weary leg,
Then *yowl*, my foot caught in a serpent's tongue.

'Twas Tom, mining under our sheets,
I kicked him hard to force him to the floor,
He yowled and fell, but won another heat,
Jumped back on to the bed and spat yet more.

My wife volleyed in from the Inner Wheel,
Grabbed for Tom, to carry him away,
He ambushed her and bit her heel,
Then stalked away to the supper tray.

We keep our bedroom door locked these days,
But the visitor's room is open, as always.

THE MIRROR IMAGE

Look in the glass and tell the face thou viewest.
Tom slunk into my lady's pink boudoir,
Where each day her hand cruel age renewest,
Where powder and paint surround the mirror.

Tom raised his leg and sprayed into the glass,
He saw a tabby leg raised, mocking him,
He pissed, and Tom faced Tom in a killer's path,
A Dorian Gray struck to abjure sin.

Tom bounded up, the powder scattered,
Another Tom pounced in the copy glass,
Then the mirror ribbons fell in tatters,
My lady entered, horror was her mask.

Had Tom another cat discovered?
Can only guilty souls find our fears uncovered?

COLD COMFORT

How like a winter has my absence been.
Euros and dollars, FTSE, Dow Jones,
Silk suits, diplomacy, bargains too keen,
Plastic and chrome, handshakes of gnomes.

Refusing my tray on my BA flight home,
I dream of a welcome of sherry and roast,
Of my wife's love, praise for company loan,
The hero returns, my Winter's a boast.

The kiss of my wife is a peck on the cheek,
The flowers of Spring are plastic and dusty,
My office let to a 'temporary' geek,
The chrome just as cold, the welcome as rusty.

But Tom makes me welcome and jumps on my knee,
But his eyes are sarcastic, as plain I can see.

A MANAGEMENT GAME

Some glory in their birth, some in their skill.
I boasted at the Rotary of my Oxford degrees,
Compared myself to Tom, born only to kill,
I wagered to change his instincts' keys.

I went to the pet shop and bought a scratch pole,
It was covered in cord and had a firm base,
I computed a model, which led to my goal,
Put Tom on the base and birdsong through the lace.

Tom tore at the pole, I was pleased with my task,
He kicked it and snarled like a weirdo,
He bolted the room, his face a wild mask,
I knew my experiment would be a zero.

Tom's conditioned by birth to destroy and slay,
I failed to reform him, though I am MBA.

THE SUCKERS

Since brass, nor stones, nor earth, nor boundless sea,
Nor trees, nor mice, nor the returning birds,
Can encompass Tom's world in its entirety.
For Tom needs us for food, we foolish nerds.

Tom sits on my knee, and I read *The Times*,
He claws the paper, in anger I roar,
I drag *The Times* as he mines from behind.
He bats *The Times* away under the sideboard.

Into the kitchen, he follows my wife,
Jumps on the surface and knocks down the fish,
My wife then prepares the cod with a knife.
Tom eats, then out with an ungrateful hiss.

The stones, earth, and trees all whisper to Tom,
The clever cat who never gets the suckers

THE MAID'S STORY

While I alone did call upon thy aid,
Trapped like a foolish virgin in a farce,
The mistress absent, leaving just the maid,
I called on you to move your tabby arse.

I tried to pass you, camped upon the stair,
Your razor claw drew red blood from my feet,
Your body grew long along your lair,
I poked you with my mop on your fat seat.

The mistress sailed in through the kitchen door,
And saw me aim my cleaning mop at Tom.
She swore at me, called me 'cat-hating whore',
And snatched that tomcat to her bosom.

She sent me away with just half pay,
Put Tom in the kitchen, Go-Cat in his tray.

PRIVATE PARTS

The parts of thee the world's eye doth view,
Calendar glamour, chocolate-box lure,
Felix and Sheba, they have talking parts too,
Bewitched by the body, entranced by the fur.

Then on the catwalk, Tom raises his tail,
Walks in a straight line, then bows to his guests,
Bare between his legs, showing that he's male,
No modest knickers, glamour model, the best.

Showing the world that glamour's fur-deep,
With his smooth, silken softness, he's so nice,
But with licentiousness to make us weep,
Beauty is prideful, fur a conduit of vice.

Tom thinks a fig leaf does not give a pass,
Glamour's a fur coat and a bare arse.

FAITHLESS SWAIN

Farewell thou art too dear for my possessing.
Faithless Tom, did thus conclude the coupling,
Gave his pregnant miss a hollow blessing,
And thus absolved himself of succouring.

So like an Alfie, Wayne, or Darren,
Tom sends swollen Miss back to her owners,
They must feed the kits; they had thought her barren,
Tom gorges on Whiskers, mice, and rats a loner.

'You are too dear, Miss, I cannot feed you,
Nor possess you,' said Tom, doing a piss,
'I can find a fur love, prettier and new,
Others can keep you, pregnant Miss.'

Tom's loving is symbolic of the men of our epoch,
With Alfie, Darren, and Wayne, the law is the cock.

ENEMIES UNREQUITED

That you were unkind befriend me now,
Scott's stuck in our cat door. He came for a fight.
Tom scratches his nose with an angry miaow,
Tom advances further, trying to bite.

Tom hisses at Scott to push himself out,
Scott wriggles forward, his arms are flaying.
The maid's in the kitchen, I am about,
We assume it's a game they are playing.

Scott's head falls down, he has no air,
His mistress comes to find him at our home.
In anger, she the cat door did tear,
And satirically threw Tom Scott's bone.

She said that next time her dog's in distress,
We should his body help and his soul bless.

FALSE ACCUSATION

Those hours that with gentle work did frame,
To tending tender plants, to Mother Nature,
Brief contrast to the managerial game,
I guard life from the despoiling creature.

I returned from office talk of sacking,
To take refuge with my plants and roses,
My horror starred, the bed betrayed hacking,
'Twas Tom, I thought. It is Tom who noses.

Tom came to court, but as a witness first,
I shouted, and he led me along the way,
To the fence, to see Scott a rosebud nurse,
Then Tom showed me the footprints in the clay.

Scott is the villain active in our street,
Tom is the hero whom the Queen will meet.

A VISIT FROM AN IMPORTANT MAN

If thy soul check thee that I come so near.
The Member of Parliament came to lunch,
My wife offered him venison pies and beer,
We listened to him to give hint or hunch.

Tom was invited as the cadet branch,
To humbly curl on a Turkish carpet,
And listen to all that was advanced,
Of Parliament and the state of the market.

The Member of Parliament patted Tom's head,
He advanced his paws and then his fur arms,
Tom scratched the MP's arm, and it bled,
My wife grabbed Tom with a cry of alarm.

The MP decided Tom would not give him his vote,
He ran from our house without a word spoke.

MY TROPHIES

When I most wink then do mine eyes best see.
Tom sleeps like a snake, stripped and sleazy,
Facing me, my flag arms flaying *The Times*,
My mouth opens, Tom winks gamely, teasy.

Through half eyes, I see my trophy twinkle,
Tom yawns, sees the trophy, winks merrily,
In dream, I am perplexed, my face a winkle,
Tom awakes and stalks the trophy stealthily.

I hear him moving and open an eye,
Sit up in my chair and feel the wisest,
I remember all the golf I played and give a sigh,
Tom and the trophy, my two precious prizes.

Tom and the trophy both wink at me,
Treasures which even in dreams I see.

AT THE VET

Let me not to the marriage of true minds,
Tom, battle-sore, with a bloody head gash,
Was taken by us to the vet, Dr Hinds,
Who examined Tom and did a head wash.

Then he wiped the head wound with tender care,
Like a mother nursing her own baby,
He sponged the fur, washing every hair,
And dressed the wound to prevent malady.

He told Tom he was a beautiful cat,
Cooed and crooned as he stroked his fur,
He put him back on the consulting mat,
And gave him injections, germs to deter.

He held Tom up fur face to cheek,
A love affair which made us weep.

THE NEIGHBOUR'S TALE

Can I compare thee to a feckless whore?
You called to him with obscene howls,
He pushed his tabby head through our cat door,
And ate the food in our cat bowls.

He prowled all-conquering round the flat,
You growled, subservient to his will,
He climbed triumphant on your back,
And left you calling from the sill.

We sometimes see him in the garden,
Ignoring you as you grow fat,
He has a pretty tortie in his harem,
The lover soon of every female cat.

But in June you will have kittens three,
For me to pet upon my knee.

NARPUSSES

For shame deny thou bearest love to any,
Now as I've told, the lustful Tom Juan,
Did love and leave Miss Cat, Caprice, and many,
Their love were echoes of his own vain self's balm.

Echo's love was killed by Narcissus,
Who fell in love with himself by the lake,
Tom loves and cherishes only one puss,
Tom worships Tom, himself, for his own sake.

The carnal curl, the leisurely lick of fur,
He courts his body so seductively,
He gives his body to the sun and purrs,
He views others' love with negativity.

Does Tom love me when he sits on my knee?
He yawns with boredom, that's all I can see.

CANDICE

From fairest creatures we desire increase.
Cafe-latte fur, her ripe body sold,
She was caged down our street, Princess Caprice.
My neighbours wished to turn her womb to gold.

She screams for a lover, hot brothel cat,
She's marked on the paw, awaiting her prince,
Her scent arrests Tom, outside where he sat.
He jumps in the window, she takes the hints.

My greedy neighbour sees Candice grow fat,
Her prince is a cuckold, her master a noddy,
Her increase is due to the charms of Tom the Cat.
No holiday in Crete will come from her body.

Two months pass, and Candice has six kits,
Six tabby toms, the delight of the wits.

TO WAX AND WANE

AS fast as thou shalt wane, so fast thou growest
My dim eyes saw a stripy knitting ball
Lying on the lawn, which I myself mowest
I thought I must the unravelling stall.

The ball became long upon the lawn
With gaudy stripes, a collar for a king
And emerald jewels, which we could pawn
To pay for Tom to learn to dance and sing.

The collar turned into a gothic arch
To herald in a colony of ants
Which in formation through the high arch marched
I almost heard the insects scream and pant.

'Twas Tom who waxed and waned along the grass,
A miracle, like the Catholic Mass.

LIEDER

Music to hear, why hearest music sadly?
Tom sprawled on the rug. The lieder played,
I saw Tom weep, while I listened gladly,
The songs of sin by Tom tearfully weighed.

Tom's eyes were running tears on to his fur,
Surprised to see him so distressed by a song,
And so sadly drawn by the music's lure,
I went to his chair to see what was wrong.

Caressing the sad eyes of my tomcat,
I wiped the tissues round his eyes,
Embedded here I found a gnat,
The cause of tears, not songs of sin and lies.

Repentance is not a theme which touches Tom,
He cries not now the gnat is gone.

THE STARS

Not from the stars do I my judgement pluck,
But from a study of the reasoning,
I minimise the random risks of luck,
See the substance, not the seasoning.

The sun and stars govern Tom's destiny,
Venus inspires his quest for love,
Mars, the dark spur of his avidity,
His soul is captive to the healing dove.

My wife read *The Sun* and said as a Leo,
She would be rich, so said the tarot cards,
I told her not to read that say-so,
Two cats run by *The Sun*, I by *Hansard*.

When at night I observe the distant stars,
I compute how to send my two cats to Mars.

EARTHLY BEAST

How can my muse want subject to invent?
Great poets write on lofty themes,
And critics argue what is meant,
My muse is elemental, Tom, my dreams.

Muslims describe how God received ten beasts,
Exemplary beasts, one Jesus's ass,
The poets praised their lofty lives at feasts,
And celebrate their spirits at mass.

Why do I find my muse in Tom?
The music of his earthly life moves me,
I need no lofty vestments to don on,
His nature played on each right key.

I need no noble subject for my poetry,
Ten Bible beasts cannot inspire me.

OLD AND BLACK

In old age black was not accounted fair,
Old Morgan crouched on our garden wall,
Tom hissed at her from his grassy lair,
Her black arm raised, she menaced with her call.

Tom the Cat advanced and jumped upon the wall,
With lowered head, he moved towards Morgan,
Morgan moved back, Tom pounced to maul,
Surely he won't hurt her even if he can.

But old and black, she was not young and ripe,
Tom punished her for age and ugliness,
And in her fury, she turned round to bite,
Tom's cheek ran rich red bloodiness.

To torment the old and black is not legal,
But Morgan's self-defence was regal.

COST/BENEFIT ANALYSIS

Thy gifts, thy tables, are within my brain,
And Tom's recorded on my database,
Each week I reassess Tom's data again,
And print out graphs, to monitor each case.

Tom's data starts from earliest time,
When primitive cats roamed on our earth,
The data in *bold*, charts from when Tom was mine,
The graphs show how he changed my purse.

I placed a value on Tom's gifts and food,
I recorded the costs and benefits,
The returns were poor. I nearly sued.
Tom's unproductive. We're just twits.

My data showed Tom is not cost-effective,
His value to me is merely subjective.

INVITATION WITHDRAWN

Whoever hath her wish hath her will,
Mrs Henley Jones visited our home,
Under a giant hat, with a voice so shrill,
She asked us to dine at the Ranger and Sloane.

She sat straight-backed on a velvet chair,
And motioned to Tom, with a gesture so curt,
He came to her feet and started to tear,
Then jumped on her knee and scratched her skirt.

Mrs Henley Jones was a battling sort,
She held off her enemy by his head,
She grabbed his arms so he was caught,
She threw him to the ground like a load of lead.

She withdrew our invitation to dinner,
And sent a bill to the feline sinner.

TOM BEATS THE CREDIT CRUNCH

When in disgrace of comfort,
Tom the Cat howls,
The car unused, the carers stay in bed,
He stops before the empty bowls and growls,
He waits all day, but rarely is he fed.

The credit crunch affects Tom too,
Two tins a week, the money's spent,
He sits by the cold fire to mew,
Cat's pay for unemployment.

And if the home is placed for auction,
And Tom is taken to a pen,
He'll slum it there with Cat Protections,
With moggies, ferals, prying women.

But clever Tom moves to the Bulls at 43,
And shares the pleasures of the rising FTSE.

RATS AND MICE

'Tis better to be vile than vile esteemed,
Tom dragged the mangled mice and rats,
To swirl in living blood where entrails teemed,
Onto the threshold where the maid took hats.

When my lady stepped through the door,
She uttered a screech of sharp dismay,
She saw vile Tom, his bloody paw,
His mouth of clown, crammed with his prey.

She screamed and shouted, 'Away, vile cat!'
Not fazed by murder, but mess upon the step,
'We want no vulgar filth upon our mat,
I wish we had brought a more elegant pet.'

So Tom now takes his haul behind the shed,
Murders unknown are words unsaid.

DUALISM

Two loves I have, of conflict and despair,
Both Tom, his dual spirit reigns supreme,
Tom's dark sky breaks, his dawn rises to repair,
He breathes soft rays into my black dreams.

Tom's fur head pushed into my library,
Where antique books are ranged by my own plan,
Tom shows a taste for Descartes's philosophy,
'I miaow, therefore I destroy. Cat I am.'

My heart sank low after the book attack,
I took to my bed with rank despair,
Tom came and lay by me, a loving cat,
My tears fell soft upon this felon's hair.

Tom nullifies the harm he does to me,
A saint, repentant, purrs upon my knee.

LIES

These lines that I have writ before do lie.
The neighbours came with a noisy basket,
With stony faces, they removed the tie,
Six tabby kits fell out across the parquet.

My neighbour demanded compensation.
Tom had seduced pedigree Candice,
I said I knew not of this fornication,
Tom was at home; he did not know this beast.

I lied for Tom, to preserve his good name.
I said it was Candice's fault, not Tom's,
I said the Fall was women's shame,
I shut the door and gathered up my Tom.

You read my verses of Tom's conquests,
And now can judge of truth's tests.

WE AGE

Unthrifty loveliness, why does thou spend?
My wife and I stood before the looking glass,
Costly costumes, false face, fragile, back bent,
Time spent, we stood as grey cracked, bent grass.

Our income rose, our beauty disappeared,
Tom stood on the shelf, around us to coil,
His tabby face between us oh-so weird,
His glossy fur and shining eyes our foil.

For time has lavishly made Tom her loans,
Our interest paid and no renewing,
Time lost for us, Tom's gamble on Dow Jones,
And we fall as weeds to love's mortgaging.

We'll stand no more before the mirror of time,
Let Tom wager for youth's last dime.

HEAVEN.COM

If thou survive my-well contented day,
And see *The Times* no longer in my hand,
The last book read, abandoned where it lay,
And see my flowers bowed in the sand.

When you fur brush my Phoenix laptop,
And see my files have died with me,
And I'll know not if FTSE is up or not,
Or never again see the news on TV.

And you will no more sit upon my knee,
Amongst the porcelain and rugs,
And hear my wife dispute with me,
Whether or not the Turkish rug has bugs.

And when I sign on *Heaven.com*,
My password will be *ILOVETOM*.

WE ARE HISTORY

Who will believe my verse in times to come?
When nuclear war has destroyed the land,
And high-tech buildings arise from the slums,
And cats are banished as an outlaw band.

And those who read my verses will show surprise,
That such a pet as Tom was by my side,
Indulgent to the creature, most unwise,
I wrote fondly of murder, vice, and lies.

They learnt that Tom plagued mistress and maid,
Fought cowardly, lost us all our contacts,
Abandoned the lady cats he had laid,
Ignored his children and all that they did lack.

Men of the future will concur that I was a prat,
Not knowing how it feels to love Tom the Cat.

TO BE ALIVE

When I do count the clock which tells the time,
I hear the fleeting music of our years,
But knowing five to yours is one to mine,
And one your joy is five my tears.

For time not wasted in a troubled youth,
You ran and climbed and found a mate,
All in one year you found your truth,
While I did wait and ponder 'till too late.

You never wasted time upon decisions, thoughts,
For seventeen years you revelled in grass, sky,
Instinctive and alive, each year brought,
Knowledge of living, but what then have I?

Are intellect and hope and fear a curse?
Does Tom live only in human verse?

Printed in the United States
By Bookmasters